@Copyright 2020by Kent Hicks- **All rights reserved.**

This document is geared towards providing exact and reliable information in regards to the topic and issue covered. The publication is sold with the idea that the publisher is not required to render accounting, officially permitted, or otherwise, qualified services. If advice is necessary, legal or professional, a practiced individual in the profession should be ordered.

Under no circumstance will any legal responsibility or blame be held against the publisher for any reparation, damages, or monetary loss due to the information herein, either directly or indirectly.

Legal Notice:

The book is copyright protected. This is only for personal use. You cannot amend, distribute, sell, use, quote or paraphrase any part or the content within this book without the consent of the author.

Disclaimer Notice:

Please note the information contained within this document is for educational and entertainment purposes only. Every attempt has been made to provide accurate, up to date and reliable complete information. No warranties of any kind are expressed or implied. Readers acknowledge that the author is not engaging in the rendering of legal, financial, medical or professional advice. The content of this book has been derived from various sources. Please consult a licensed professional before attempting any techniques outlined in this book.

CONTENTS

Chapter 1: Breakfast 4
    Delightful Spiced Up Cauliflower 4
    Fine Fried Eggs 5
    Morning Carrot Puree 6
    Zucchini Egg Muffins 7
    Avocado Cream Eggs 8
    Blueberry Muffins 9
    Classic Egg Bacon Breakfast 10
    Healthy Apple Oats 11
    Hearty Broccoli Florets 12
    Nut Packed Crunchy Porridge 13

Chapter 2: Vegetarian And Vegan Recipes 14
    Cauliflower Delight 14
    Tofu And Mushrooms Crisps 15
    Broccoli Pasta Mania 16
    Spiced Chickpeas Rice 17
    Classic Leek Potato Soup 18
    Brown Rice Tofu Meal 19
    Broccoli Cream Soup 20
    Spinach Olive Meal 21
    Asparagus Meal 22
    Delicious Avocado Chips 23
    Garlic And Carrot Meal 24

Chapter 3: Chicken And Poultry Recipes 25
    The Orignial Bruschetta Chicken 25
    Lemon And Artichoke Chicken 26
    Salty Baked Chicken 27
    Tender Chicken with Cheese Sauce 28
    Turkey Spiced 29
    Classic Roasted Chicken 30
    Cream Tomato Chicken 31
    Cauliflower Chicken Meal 33
    Garlic And Lemon Chicken 34
    Hassle Chicken 35

Chapter 4: Fish And Seafood Recipes 36
    Cool Sweet Fish 36
    Shrimp Zoodles 37
    Easy Fish Stew 38
    Buttery Scallops 39
    Lovely Air Fried Scallops 40
    Sweet And Sour Fish 41
    Panko Cod Delight 42
    Salmon And Kale Meal 43
    Lemon And Garlic Flavored Prawn Dish 44

Chapter 5: Beef And Lamb Recipes 45
    Mustard Dreged Pork 45
    Jamaican Pork Dish 46
    Tantalizing Beef Jerky 47
    Spicy Adobo Steak 48
    Beef Stew 49
    Lamb Roast 50
    Mustard Pork 51
    Deliciously Smothered Pork Chops 52
    Beef And Broccoli Meal 53
    Hearty New York Strip 54

Chapter 6: Dessert 55
- Simple Poached Pears 55
- Buttery Fennel And Garlic 56
- Cheesy Cauliflower Steak 57
- Garlic And Mushroom Munchies 58
- Warm Glazed Up Carrots 59

Chapter 7: Appetizers & Sides 60
- Cauliflower Cheddar 60
- Bacon Green Beans 61
- Zucchini Crisp 62
- Butter Brussels Sprouts 63
- Parmesan Squash 64

Chapter 8: Dessert 65
- Decadent Lemon Mousse 65
- Pumpkin Carrot Pudding 66
- Awesome Poached Pears 67

Chapter 1: Breakfast

Delightful Spiced Up Cauliflower

Prep Time: 5 minutes
Cooking Time: 10 minutes
Number of Servings: 4

Ingredients:

- 1 large cauliflower, cut into florets
- 1 lemon, quartered
- 1 cup cilantro, chopped
- 2 teaspoons paprika
- 2 tablespoons olive oil
- 2 teaspoons cumin, grounded
- ¾ teaspoon salt

Method:

1. Add 1 and ½ cups water and place a steamer rack in your Ninja Foodi
2. Trim the core of the cauliflower head and cut into florets
3. Take a small bowl and mix with olive oil, salt, cumin, and paprika, then drizzle over cauliflower
4. Close the lid
5. Cook for 4 minutes on High
6. Quick-release the pressure
7. Garnish with cilantro
8. Serve and enjoy!

Nutritional Values (Per Serving)

Calories: 70 Fat: 6g Saturated Fat: 1 g Carbohydrates: 1 g Fiber: 0 g Sodium: 760 mg Protein: 3g

Fine Fried Eggs

Prep Time: 5 minutes
Cooking Time: 10 minutes
Number of Servings: 4

Ingredients:

- 4 eggs
- ¼ teaspoon ground black pepper
- 1 teaspoon butter, melted
- ¾ teaspoon salt

Method:

1. Take a small egg pan and brush it with butter.
2. Beat the eggs in the pan
3. Sprinkle with the ground black pepper and salt
4. Transfer the egg pan in the pot
5. Lower the air fryer lid
6. Cook the meat for 10 minutes at 350 F
7. Serve immediately and enjoy!

Nutritional Values (Per Serving)

Calories: 143 Fat: 10g Saturated Fat: 3 g Carbohydrates: 0.9 g Fiber: 0 g Sodium: 260 mg Protein: 11g

Morning Carrot Puree

Prep Time: 10 minutes
Cooking Time: 4 minutes
Number of Servings: 4

Ingredients:
- 1 and a ½ pound carrots, chopped
- 1 tablespoon of butter at room temperature
- 1 tablespoon of agave nectar
- ¼ teaspoon of sea salt
- 1 cup of water

Method:
1. Clean and peel your carrots properly
2. Roughly chop up them into small pieces
3. Add 1 cup of water to your Pot
4. Place the carrots in a steamer basket and place the basket in the Ninja Foodi
5. Lock up the lid and cook on HIGH pressure for 4 minutes
6. Perform a quick release
7. Transfer the carrots to a deep bowl and use an immersion blender to blend the carrots
8. Add butter, nectar, salt, and puree
9. Taste the puree and season more if needed
10. Enjoy!

Nutritional Values (Per Serving)
Calories: 143 Fat: 9g Saturated Fat: 3 g Carbohydrates: 016 g Fiber: 2 g Sodium: 571 mg Protein: 2g

Zucchini Egg Muffins

Prep Time: 5-10 min.
Cooking Time: 7 min.
Number of Servings: 4

Ingredients:
- ½ teaspoon salt
- 1 teaspoon butter
- 1 zucchini, grated
- 2 tablespoons almond flour
- 4 eggs

Method:
1. In a mixing bowl, add the almond flour, zucchini, and salt. Combine the ingredients to mix well with each other.
2. Grease the muffin molds with some butter and add the zucchini mixture in them.
3. Take Ninja Foodi multi-cooker, arrange it over a cooking platform, and open the top lid.
4. In the pot, arrange a reversible rack and place the muffin molds over.
5. Seal the multi-cooker by locking it with the crisping lid; ensure to keep the pressure release valve locked/sealed.
6. Select the "AIR CRISP" mode and adjust the 375°F temperature level. Then, set timer to 7 minutes and press "STOP/START"; it will start the cooking process by building up inside pressure. Cook until the eggs are solid.
7. When the timer goes off, quick release pressure by adjusting the pressure valve to the VENT.
8. After pressure gets released, open the pressure lid. Serve warm and enjoy!

Nutritional Values (Per Serving):
Calories: 94 Fat: 8g Saturated Fat: 1.5g Trans Fat: 0g Carbohydrates: 2.5g Fiber: 0.5g Sodium: 209mg Protein: 7g

Avocado Cream Eggs

Prep Time: 5-10 min.   **Cooking Time: 15 min.**   **Number of Servings: 4-5**

Ingredients:

- 4 eggs
- 1 teaspoon paprika
- ½ teaspoon ground black pepper
- 1 sweet bell pepper, seeded and diced
- 2 cups water
- 1 avocado, pitted and chopped
- 1 teaspoon salt
- 3 ounces lettuce leaves
- 3 tablespoons heavy cream

Method:

1. Take Ninja Foodi multi-cooker, arrange it over a cooking platform, and open the top lid.
2. In the pot, add the water and eggs.
3. Seal the multi-cooker by locking it with the pressure lid; ensure to keep the pressure release valve locked/sealed.
4. Select "PRESSURE" mode and select the "HI" pressure level. Then, set timer to 15 minutes and press "STOP/START"; it will start the cooking process by building up inside pressure.
5. When the timer goes off, quick release pressure by adjusting the pressure valve to the VENT. After pressure gets released, open the pressure lid.
6. Peel the eggs and chop them; add in a mixing bowl. Add the pepper and avocado. Sprinkle with the paprika, ground black pepper, salt,
7. Arrange the lettuce leaves, add the mixture over them and top with the cream, and serve fresh.

Nutritional Values (Per Serving):

Calories: 197 Fat: 13.5g Saturated Fat: 2g Trans Fat: 0g Carbohydrates: 6.5g Fiber: 2g Sodium: 238mg Protein: 7g

Blueberry Muffins

Prep Time: 5-10 min.
Cooking Time: 10 min.
Number of Servings: 6

Ingredients:

- ¼ cup coconut oil, melted
- 3 eggs
- 2 cups water
- 1 ¼ cups almond flour
- ½ tablespoon baking powder
- Pinch salt
- 1 teaspoon vanilla extract
- 1 tablespoon stevia or sweetener of choice (optional)
- ½ cup blueberries

Method:

1. Grease 6 muffin molds with some butter.
2. In a mixing bowl, add the almond flour, baking powder, salt, coconut oil, eggs, vanilla, and stevia. Combine the ingredients to mix well with each other.
3. Mix in the blueberries and add the mixture into muffin liners.
4. Take Ninja Foodi multi-cooker, arrange it over a cooking platform, and open the top lid.
5. In the pot, arrange a reversible rack and place the muffin molds.
6. Seal the multi-cooker by locking it with the pressure lid; ensure to keep the pressure release valve locked/sealed.
7. Select "PRESSURE" mode and select the "LOW" pressure level. Then, set timer to 10 minutes and press "STOP/START"; it will start the cooking process by building up inside pressure.
8. When the timer goes off, naturally release inside pressure for about 8-10 minutes. Then, quick-release pressure by adjusting the pressure valve to the VENT. Serve warm and enjoy!

Nutritional Values (Per Serving):

Calories: 246   Fat: 19.5g   Saturated Fat: 3g   Trans Fat: 0g   Carbohydrates: 9.5g   Fiber: 3.5g   Sodium: 382mg   Protein: 7.5g

Classic Egg Bacon Breakfast

Prep Time: 5-10 min.   **Cooking Time: 8 min.**   **Number of Servings: 2**

Ingredients:

1 tablespoon chopped parsley

2 medium eggs, whisked

2 cooked bacon strips, chopped

Black pepper and salt to the taste

Method:

1. In a mixing bowl, beat the eggs. One by one, add other ingredients and combine well.
2. Take a baking pan or cake pan; grease it with some cooking spray, vegetable oil, or butter.
3. Add the egg mixture and wrap the pan with aluminum foil.
4. Take Ninja Foodi multi-cooker, arrange it over a cooking platform, and open the top lid.
5. In the pot, add water and place a reversible rack inside the pot. Place the pan over the rack.
6. Seal the multi-cooker by locking it with the crisping lid; ensure to keep the pressure release valve locked/sealed.
7. Select "BAKE/ROAST" mode and adjust the 400°F temperature level. Then, set timer to 8 minutes and press "STOP/START"; it will start the cooking process by building up inside pressure.
8. When the timer goes off, quick release pressure by adjusting the pressure valve to the VENT. After pressure gets released, open the pressure lid.
9. Serve warm and enjoy!

Nutritional Values (Per Serving):

Calories: 135 Fat: 10g Saturated Fat: 4.5g Trans Fat: 0g Carbohydrates: 1g   Fiber: 0g Sodium: 458mg Protein: 9g

Healthy Apple Oats

Prep Time: 5-10 min.
Cooking Time: 11 min.
Number of Servings: 4

Ingredients:
- ¼ cup apple cider vinegar
- ½ teaspoon vanilla extract
- 1 tablespoon ground cinnamon
- ½ teaspoon ground nutmeg
- 2 cups steel-cut oats
- 2 apples, peeled, cored, and diced
- 3 ¾ cups water
- ½ cup dried cranberries
- ⅛ teaspoon sea salt
- Maple syrup to taste

Method:
1. Take Ninja Foodi multi-cooker, arrange it over a cooking platform, and open the top lid.
2. In the pot, add the oats, water, vinegar, cinnamon, nutmeg, vanilla, cranberries, apples, and salt.
3. Seal the multi-cooker by locking it with the pressure lid; ensure to keep the pressure release valve locked/sealed.
4. Select "PRESSURE" mode and select the "HI" pressure level. Then, set timer to 11 minutes and press "STOP/START"; it will start the cooking process by building up inside pressure.
5. When the timer goes off, naturally release inside pressure for about 8-10 minutes. Then, quick-release pressure by adjusting the pressure valve to the VENT.
6. After pressure gets released, open the pressure lid.
7. Serve warm with the maple syrup and some berries on top.

Nutritional Values (Per Serving):
Calories: 374 Fat: 6.5g Saturated Fat: 1g Trans Fat: 0g Carbohydrates: 52.5g Fiber: 9g Sodium: 103mg Protein: 14g

Hearty Broccoli Florets

Prep Time: 10 minutes
Cooking Time: 6 minutes
Number of Servings: 4

Ingredients:
- 4 tablespoons butter, melted
- Salt and pepper to taste
- 2 pounds broccoli florets
- 1 cup whipping cream

Method:
1. Place a steamer basket in your Ninja Foodi (bottom part) and add water
2. Place florets on top of the basket and lock lid
3. Cook on HIGH pressure for 5 minutes
4. Quick-release pressure
5. Transfer florets from the steamer basket to the pot
6. Add salt, pepper, butter, and stir
7. Lock crisping lid and cook on Air Crisp mode for 360 degrees F
8. Serve and enjoy!

Nutritional Values (Per Serving)
Calories: 178 Fat: 14g Saturated Fat: 4 g Carbohydrates: 8 g Fiber: 2 g Sodium: 180 mg Protein: 5g

Nut Packed Crunchy Porridge

Prep Time: 10 minutes
Cooking Time: 10 minutes
Number of Servings: 6

Ingredients:

- 1 cup pecans, halved
- 1 cup cashew nuts, raw and unsalted
- 4 teaspoons coconut oil, melted
- 2 cups of water

Method:

1. Add 1 and ½ cups water and place a steamer rack in your Ninja Foodi
2. Trim the core of the cauliflower head and cut into florets
3. Take a small bowl and mix with olive oil, salt, cumin, and paprika, then drizzle over cauliflower
4. Close the lid
5. Cook for 4 minutes on High
6. Quick-release the pressure
7. Garnish with cilantro
8. Serve and enjoy!

Nutritional Values (Per Serving)

Calories: 70 Fat: 6g Saturated Fat: g Carbohydrates: 1 g Fiber: 0 g Sodium: 79 mg Protein: 3g

Chapter 2: Vegetarian And Vegan Recipes

Cauliflower Delight

Prep Time: 10 minutes
Cooking Time: 35 minutes
Number of Servings: 6

Ingredients:
- 1 head cauliflower
- ½ cup parmesan cheese, grated
- 1 tablespoon mustard, Keto-Friendly
- 1 teaspoon avocado mayonnaise
- ¼ cup butter, cut into small pieces

Method:
1. Set your Ninja Foodi to Saute mode
2. Add butter and melt it
3. Add cauliflower and saute for 3 minutes
4. Add rest of the ingredients and close the lid
5. Cook for 30 minutes on High
6. Release pressure naturally over 10 minutes
7. Serve and enjoy!

Nutritional Values (Per Serving)
Calories: 155 Fat: 13g Saturated Fat: 2 g Carbohydrates: 2g Fiber: 0 g Sodium: 560 mg Protein: 7g

Tofu And Mushrooms Crisps

Prep Time: 10 minutes
Cooking Time: 10 minutes
Number of Servings: 4

Ingredients:

- 8 tablespoons parmesan cheese, shredded
- 2 cups fresh mushrooms, chopped
- 2 blocks tofu, pressed and cubed
- Salt and pepper to taste
- 8 tablespoons butter

Method:

1. Take a bowl and mix in tofu, salt, and pepper
2. Set your Ninja Foodi to Saute mode and add seasoned tofu, Saute for 5 minutes
3. Add mushroom, cheese and Saute for 3 minutes
4. Lock crisping lid and Air Crisp for 3 minutes at 350 degrees F
5. Transfer to a serving plate and enjoy!

Nutritional Values (Per Serving)

Calories: 211 Fat: 18g Saturated Fat: 6 g Carbohydrates: 2 g Fiber: 1 g Sodium: 427 mg Protein: 11g

Broccoli Pasta Mania

Prep Time: 5-10 min.
Cooking Time: 15 min.
Number of Servings: 4

Ingredients:
- 3 tablespoons olive oil
- 3 teaspoons kosher salt
- 10 ounces fettucine pasta, broken in half
- 1 bunch asparagus, trimmed, cut into 1-inch pieces
- 2 cups small broccoli florets
- 3 garlic cloves, minced
- 2 ½ cups water
- ½ cup grated Parmesan cheese
- ¼ cup chopped parsley or basil
- ½ cup heavy whipping cream
- 1 cup cherry tomatoes, halved

Method:
1. Take Ninja Foodi multi-cooker, arrange it over a cooking platform, and open the top lid.
2. In the pot, arrange a reversible rack and place the Crisping Basket over the rack.
3. In the basket, add the asparagus and broccoli. Add 1 tablespoon olive oil and ½ teaspoon of kosher salt; stir the mixture.
4. Seal the multi-cooker by locking it with the crisping lid; ensure to keep the pressure release valve locked/sealed.
5. Select the "AIR CRISP" mode and adjust the 375°F temperature level. Then, set timer to 2 minutes and press "STOP/START"; it will start the cooking process by building up inside pressure.
6. When the timer goes off, quick release pressure by adjusting the pressure valve to the VENT.
7. After pressure gets released, open the pressure lid. Set aside the basket.
8. In the pot, add the pasta and remaining oil. Stir to coat evenly.
9. Add remaining kosher salt, garlic, and water.
10. Seal the multi-cooker by locking it with the pressure lid; ensure to keep the pressure release valve locked/sealed.
11. Select "PRESSURE" mode and select the "HI" pressure level. Then, set timer to 5 minutes and press "STOP/START"; it will start the cooking process by building up inside pressure.
12. When the timer goes off, quick release pressure by adjusting the pressure valve to VENT. After pressure gets released, open the pressure lid.
13. Select "SEAR/SAUTÉ" mode and select the "MD" pressure level; add the heavy cream and tomatoes. Stir-cook until the sauce thickens.
14. Add the broccoli and asparagus; serve with some herbs and cheese on top.

Nutritional Values (Per Serving):
Calories: 524 Fat: 24.5g Saturated Fat: 10.5g Trans Fat: 0g Carbohydrates: 51.5g Fiber: 5g Sodium: 626mg Protein: 17.5g

Spiced Chickpeas Rice

Prep Time: 5-10 min.
Cooking Time: 18 min.
Number of Servings: 6-8

Ingredients:
- 6 garlic cloves, minced
- 28 ounce canned tomatoes, chopped
- 14 ounce coconut milk
- 1 pound chickpeas
- 1 yellow onion, chopped
- A pinch of black pepper and salt
- 1 bunch cilantro, chopped
- 4 tablespoons coconut oil
- 1 tablespoons grated ginger
- 1 green chili pepper, chopped
- 2 ½ cups water
- 2 teaspoon garam masala or spice mix
- 2 teaspoon sugar
- 1 teaspoon chili powder
- 1 teaspoon turmeric powder
- 1 tablespoons cumin, ground
- Juice of 2 lemons
- Cooked rice to serve

Method:
1. Take Ninja Foodi multi-cooker, arrange it over a cooking platform, and open the top lid.
2. In the pot, add the oil; Select "SEAR/SAUTÉ" mode and select "MD: HI" pressure level.
3. Press "STOP/START." After about 4-5 minutes, the oil will start simmering.
4. Add the onions, cumin, black pepper, and salt; cook (while stirring) until it becomes softened and translucent for about 4 minutes.
5. Add the turmeric, garlic, ginger, chili, chili powder, and cilantro, stir-cook for 2 minutes.
6. Add the tomatoes, water, coconut milk and chickpeas; combine again.
7. Seal the multi-cooker by locking it with the pressure lid; ensure to keep the pressure release valve locked/sealed.
8. Select "PRESSURE" mode and select the "LO" pressure level. Then, set timer to 10 minutes and press "STOP/START"; it will start the cooking process by building up inside pressure.
9. When the timer goes off, naturally release inside pressure for about 8-10 minutes. Then, quick-release pressure by adjusting the pressure valve to VENT.
10. Select "SEAR/SAUTÉ" mode and select the "MD" pressure level; add the sugar, garam masala, and lemon juice. Stir-cook for 4 minutes.
11. Serve warm with cooked rice.

Nutritional Values (Per Serving):
Calories: 201 Fat: 11.5g Saturated Fat: 1g Trans Fat: 0g Carbohydrates: 21g Fiber: 4g Sodium: 589mg Protein: 13.5g

Classic Leek Potato Soup

Prep Time: 5-10 min.
Cooking Time: 15 min.
Number of Servings: 5-6

Ingredients:
- 4 garlic cloves, minced
- 5 Yukon Gold potatoes, peeled
- 2 tablespoons extra-virgin olive oil
- 4 leeks, cleaned and thinly sliced
- 5 cups vegetable broth
- ¾ cup white wine
- 1 ½ cups light cream
- ½ cup grated Cheddar cheese
- 3 thyme sprigs, stems removed
- 2 bay leaves
- ½ teaspoon ground black pepper
- 1 ½ teaspoons dried oregano
- 1 teaspoon sea salt

Method:
1. Take Ninja Foodi multi-cooker, arrange it over a cooking platform, and open the top lid. In the pot, add the oil; Select "SEAR/SAUTÉ" mode and select "MD: HI" pressure level.
2. Press "STOP/START." After about 4-5 minutes, the oil will start simmering.
3. Add 3/4th leeks and cook (while stirring) until turn softened for 4-5 minutes.
4. Add the garlic and cook for 1 minute.
5. Add the potatoes, thyme, bay leaves, vegetable broth, white wine, oregano, salt, and black pepper; combine well.
6. Seal the multi-cooker by locking it with the pressure lid; ensure to keep the pressure release valve locked/sealed.
7. Select "PRESSURE" mode and select the "HI" pressure level. Then, set timer to 10 minutes and press "STOP/START"; it will start the cooking process by building up inside pressure.
8. When the timer goes off, quick release pressure by adjusting the pressure valve to VENT. After pressure gets released, open the pressure lid.
9. Take out the bay leaves; add the cream and mash to make a smooth mixture. Add the cheese on top.
10. In a mixing bowl, add the remaining leeks and remaining oil.
11. In the pot, add the reversible rack and place the leeks on top.
12. Seal the multi-cooker by locking it with the crisping lid; ensure to keep the pressure release valve locked/sealed.
13. Select "BROIL" mode and select the "HI" pressure level. Then, set timer to 5 minutes and press "STOP/START"; it will start the cooking process by building up inside pressure.
14. When the timer goes off, quick release pressure by adjusting the pressure valve to VENT.
15. After pressure gets released, open the pressure lid.
16. Serve the soup with the leeks on top.

Nutritional Values (Per Serving):
Calories: 372 Fat: 19g Saturated Fat: 8g Trans Fat: 0g Carbohydrates: 48g Fiber: 3.5g Sodium: 852mg Protein: 9g

Brown Rice Tofu Meal

Prep Time: 5-10 min.
Cooking Time: 30 min.
Number of Servings: 4

Ingredients:
- 1 sweet potato, peeled and diced
- 2 tablespoons extra-virgin olive oil
- 1 cup brown rice, rinsed
- ¾ cup water
- 1 teaspoon black pepper, freshly ground
- 1 teaspoon sea salt
- 1 (15-ounce) block extra-firm tofu, drained and cut into small cubes
- 2 teaspoons cornstarch
- 1 tablespoon soy sauce

Method:
1. In a mixing bowl, add the sweet potato, salt, black pepper, and coat with one tablespoon of olive oil.
2. In another mixing bowl, add remaining olive oil and soy sauce. Add the tofu and toss well. Add the cornstarch and stir until evenly coated.
3. Take Ninja Foodi multi-cooker, arrange it over a cooking platform, and open the top lid.
4. In the pot, add the water and rice.
5. Seal the multi-cooker by locking it with the pressure lid; ensure to keep the pressure release valve locked/sealed.
6. Select "PRESSURE" mode and select the "HI" pressure level. Then, set timer to 2 minutes and press "STOP/START"; it will start the cooking process by building up inside pressure.
7. When the timer goes off, quick release pressure by adjusting the pressure valve to the VENT. After pressure gets released, open the pressure lid.
8. In the pot, place a reversible rack inside the pot. Place the sweet potatoes and tofu over the rack.
9. Seal the multi-cooker by locking it with the crisping lid; ensure to keep the pressure release valve locked/sealed.
10. Select the "AIR CRISP" mode and adjust the 400°F temperature level. Then, set timer to 20 minutes and press "STOP/START"; it will start the cooking process by building up inside pressure.
11. When the timer goes off, quick release pressure by adjusting the pressure valve to the VENT.
12. After pressure gets released, open the pressure lid.
13. Serve warm with the cooked rice and enjoy!

Nutritional Values (Per Serving):
Calories: 316 Fat: 10g Saturated Fat: 2.5g Trans Fat: 0g Carbohydrates: 41g Fiber: 4g Sodium: 924mg Protein: 12g

Broccoli Cream Soup

Prep Time: 5-10 min.
Cooking Time: 10 min.
Number of Servings: 4

Ingredients:

- 1 head broccoli, cut into florets
- 4 cups vegetable broth
- 2 ½ pounds potatoes, peeled and chopped
- ½ cup heavy cream
- ⅓ cup butter, melted
- 1 onion, chopped
- 2 cloves garlic, minced
- ½ cup chopped scallions
- Ground black pepper and salt to taste
- Cheddar cheese to serve

Method:

1. Take Ninja Foodi multi-cooker, arrange it over a cooking platform, and open the top lid.
2. In the pot, add the butter; Select "SEAR/SAUTÉ" mode and select "MD: HI" pressure level.
3. Press "STOP/START." After about 4-5 minutes, the butter will start simmering.
4. Add the onions, garlic, and cook (while stirring) for 3-4 minutes until they become softened and translucent.
5. Add the broth, potatoes, and broccoli and mix well.
6. Seal the multi-cooker by locking it with the pressure lid; ensure to keep the pressure release valve locked/sealed.
7. Select "PRESSURE" mode and select the "HI" pressure level. Then, set timer to 5 minutes and press "STOP/START"; it will start the cooking process by building up inside pressure.
8. When the timer goes off, quick release pressure by adjusting the pressure valve to the VENT. After pressure gets released, open the pressure lid.
9. Add the potato mixture in a blender and blend well to puree the mixture. Add the heavy cream and season with pepper and salt to taste; combine well.
10. Serve with scallions and cheese on top.

Nutritional Values (Per Serving):

Calories: 549 Fat: 27.5g Saturated Fat: 8g Trans Fat: 0g Carbohydrates: 36g Fiber: 9.5g Sodium: 547mg Protein: 19g

Spinach Olive Meal

Prep Time: 5-10 min.
Cooking Time: 15 min.
Number of Servings: 5-6

Ingredients:

- 2/3 cup Kalamata olives, halved and pitted
- 1 ½ cups feta cheese, grated
- 4 tablespoons butter
- 2 pounds spinach, chopped and boiled
- Ground black pepper and salt to taste
- 4 teaspoons grated lemon zest

Method:

1. In a mixing bowl, add the spinach, butter, salt, pepper.
2. Take Ninja Foodi multi-cooker, arrange it over a cooking platform, and open the top lid.
3. In the pot, arrange a reversible rack and place the Crisping Basket over the rack.
4. In the basket, add the spinach mixture.
5. Seal the multi-cooker by locking it with the crisping lid; ensure to keep the pressure release valve locked/sealed.
6. Select the "AIR CRISP" mode and adjust the 340°F temperature level. Then, set timer to 15 minutes and press "STOP/START"; it will start the cooking process by building up inside pressure.
7. When the timer goes off, quick release pressure by adjusting the pressure valve to the VENT.
8. After pressure gets released, open the pressure lid.
9. Serve warm and enjoy!

Nutritional Values (Per Serving):

Calories: 253 Fat: 18g Saturated Fat: 3g Trans Fat: 0g Carbohydrates: 8g Fiber: 4g Sodium: 339mg Protein: 10.5g

Asparagus Meal

Prep Time: 10 minutes
Cooking Time: 10 minutes
Number of Servings: 4

Ingredients:

- 1 cup asparagus
- ½ cup coconut, desiccated
- ½ cup feta cheese

Method:

1. Add coconut in a shallow dish, coat asparagus with coconut
2. Transfer to Ninja Foodi and top with feta cheese
3. Lock Crisping lid and Air Crisp for 10 minutes at 360 degrees F
4. Serve and enjoy!

Nutritional Values (Per Serving)

Calories: 133 Fat: 10g Saturated Fat: 4 g Carbohydrates: 5 g Fiber: 2 g Sodium: 814 mg Protein: 7 g

Delicious Avocado Chips

Prep Time: 10 minutes
Cooking Time: 10 minutes
Number of Servings: 4

Ingredients:
- 4 tablespoons butter
- 4 raw avocados, peeled and sliced in chips
- Salt and pepper to taste

Method:
1. Season avocado slices with salt and pepper
2. Grease pot of Ninja Foodi with butter and add the avocado slices
3. Air Crisp for 10 minutes at 350 degrees F
4. Remove from Foodi and transfer to a plate
5. Serve and enjoy!

Nutritional Values (Per Serving)
Calories: 391 Fat: 38g Saturated Fat: 8 g Carbohydrates: 15 g Fiber: 3 g Sodium: 450 mg Protein: 3.5 g

Garlic And Carrot Meal

Prep Time: 10 minutes
Cooking Time: 10-15 minutes
Number of Servings: 4

Ingredients:
- 3 cups carrots, chopped
- 1 tablespoon melted butter
- 1 cup of water
- ½ teaspoon garlic salt
- 1 tablespoon fresh dill, minced

Method:
1. Add all ingredients to your Ninja Foodi
2. Stir and lock the lid
3. Cook on High for 10 minutes
4. Quick-release pressure
5. Serve with dill on top
6. Enjoy!

Nutritional Values (Per Serving)

Calories: 207 Fat: 16g Saturated Fat: 4 g Carbohydrates: 5g Fiber: 3 g Sodium: 501 mg Protein: 8g

Chapter 3: Chicken And Poultry Recipes

The Orignial Bruschetta Chicken

Prep Time: 5 minutes
Cooking Time: 9 minutes
Number of Servings: 4

Ingredients:

- 2 pounds chicken breasts, quartered, boneless
- ½ cup sun-dried tomatoes, in olive oil
- 2 tablespoons balsamic vinegar
- 1/3 cup olive oil
- 2 teaspoons garlic cloves, minced
- 1 teaspoon black pepper
- 2 tablespoons fresh basil, chopped
- ½ teaspoon salt

Method:
1. In a bowl add garlic, pepper, vinegar, oil, and salt
2. Whisk them well
3. Place it in your fridge and keep for 30 minutes
4. Add everything to Ninja Foodi and close the lid
5. Cook for 20 minutes on Low
6. Quick-release the pressure
7. Serve and enjoy!

Nutritional Values (Per Serving)
Calories: 480g Fat: 26g Saturated Fat: 8 g Carbohydrates: 4g Fiber: 1 g Sodium: 856 mg Protein: 52g

Lemon And Artichoke Chicken

Prep Time: 10 minutes
Cooking Time: 8 hours
Number of Servings: 4

Ingredients:

- 1 pound boneless and skinless chicken breast
- 1 pound boneless and skinless chicken thigh
- 14 ounces (can) artichoke hearts, packed in water and drained
- 1 onion, diced
- 2 carrots, diced
- 3 garlic cloves, minced
- 1 bay leaf
- ½ teaspoon pepper
- 3 cups turnips, peeled and cubed
- 6 cups chicken broth
- 14 cup fresh lemon juice
- ¼ cup parsley, chopped

Method:

1. Add the above-mentioned ingredients to your Ninja Foodi except for lemon juice and parsley
2. Cook on Slow Cooker (LOW) for 8 hours
3. Remove the chicken and shred it up
4. Return it to the Ninja Foodi
5. Season with some pepper and salt!
6. Stir in parsley and lemon juice and serve!

Nutritional Values (Per Serving)

Calories: 400 Fat: 10g Saturated Fat: 3 g Carbohydrates: 12 g Fiber: 4 g Sodium: 316 mg Protein: 3 g

Salty Baked Chicken

Prep Time: 10 minutes
Cooking Time: 30 minutes
Number of Servings: 4

Ingredients:
- 2 teaspoons ginger, minced
- 1 and ¼ teaspoons salt
- ¼ teaspoons five-spice powder
- Dash of white pepper
- 5-6 chicken legs

Method:
1. Season the chicken legs by placing them in a large mixing bowl
2. Pour 2 teaspoon of ginger, 1 and a ¼ teaspoon of kosher salt, ¼ teaspoon of five-spice powder and mix
3. Transfer them to a parchment paper
4. Wrap up tightly and place them to a shallow dish
5. Place a steamer rack in your Ninja Foodi and add 1 cup of water
6. Place the chicken dish onto the rack
7. Lock up the lid and cook on HIGH pressure for 18-26 minutes
8. Release the pressure naturally
9. Open the lid and unwrap the paper
10. Pour the juice into a small bowl
11. Transfer the chicken on a wire rack and broil for a while
12. Serve immediately with the cooking liquid used as a dipping sauce

Nutritional Values (Per Serving)
Calories: 353 Fat: 25g Saturated Fat: 10 g Carbohydrates: 6 g Fiber: 3 g Sodium: 536 mg Protein: 26 g

Tender Chicken with Cheese Sauce

Prep Time: 5-10 min.
Cooking Time: 15 min.
Number of Servings: 4

Ingredients:
- 1 small white onion, diced
- 2 tablespoons almond flour
- 1 ½ cups chicken broth
- 2 tablespoon olive oil
- 4 chicken breasts, boneless and skinless
- Black pepper (ground) and salt to taste
- 2 teaspoons chopped thyme leaves
- 1 tablespoon chopped parsley to garnish
- ½ cup grated Asiago cheese

Method:
1. Season the chicken with salt and black pepper.
2. Take Ninja Foodi multi-cooker, arrange it over a cooking platform, and open the top lid.
3. In the pot, add the oil; Select "SEAR/SAUTÉ" mode and select "MD: HI" pressure level. Press "STOP/START." After about 4-5 minutes, the oil will start simmering.
4. Add the meat and stir cook for about 7-8 minutes to brown evenly. Set aside the chicken.
5. Add the onions and cook (while stirring) until they become softened and translucent.
6. Add the almond flour and stir. Add the chicken broth, thyme, and cook until the sauce reduces by one-third quantity. Stir in the cheese until melts. Add back the chicken and coat well.
7. Seal the multi-cooker by locking it with the pressure lid; ensure to keep the pressure release valve locked/sealed.
8. Select "PRESSURE" mode and select the "HI" pressure level. Then, set timer to 3 minutes and press "STOP/START"; it will start the cooking process by building up inside pressure.
9. When the timer goes off, naturally release inside pressure for about 8-10 minutes. Then, quick-release pressure by adjusting the pressure valve to the VENT. Serve warm with the parsley on top and enjoy!

Nutritional Values (Per Serving):
Calories: 603 Fat: 32.5g Saturated Fat: 8.5g Trans Fat: 0g Carbohydrates: 4g Fiber: 1.5g Sodium: 1054mg Protein: 58g

Turkey Spiced

Prep Time: 5-10 min.
Cooking Time: 13 min.
Number of Servings: 4

Ingredients:

- 2 garlic cloves, minced
- 1 tablespoon dried oregano
- 1 tablespoon ground coriander
- 4 cups chicken broth
- 1 tablespoon olive oil
- 1 onion, chopped
- 1 ½ pounds ground turkey
- ⅛ teaspoon salt
- ⅛ teaspoon black pepper (ground)

Method:

1. Take Ninja Foodi multi-cooker, arrange it over a cooking platform, and open the top lid.
2. In the pot, add the oil; Select "SEAR/SAUTÉ" mode and select "MD: HI" pressure level.
3. Press "STOP/START." After about 4-5 minutes, the oil will start simmering.
4. Add the onions, garlic, and cook (while stirring) until they become softened and translucent for 2-3 minutes.
5. Add the oregano, coriander, turkey, and chicken broth; stir the mixture.
6. Seal the multi-cooker by locking it with the pressure lid; ensure to keep the pressure release valve locked/sealed.
7. Select "PRESSURE" mode and select the "HI" pressure level. Then, set timer to 10 minutes and press "STOP/START"; it will start the cooking process by building up inside pressure.
8. When the timer goes off, quick release pressure by adjusting the pressure valve to the VENT. After pressure gets released, open the pressure lid. Season to taste with salt and black pepper.
9. Serve warm with cauliflower rice (optional) and enjoy!

Nutritional Values (Per Serving):

Calories: 317   Fat: 18g   Saturated Fat: 3.5g   Trans Fat: 0g   Carbohydrates: 4.5g   Fiber: 1g   Sodium: 658mg   Protein: 38g

Classic Roasted Chicken

Prep Time: 5-10 min.
Cooking Time: 40 min.
Number of Servings: 4

Ingredients:
- 1 teaspoon garlic powder
- 1 teaspoon onion powder
- ½ cup water
- 1 (4 ½ pound) whole chicken
- Black pepper (ground) and salt to taste
- 2 tablespoons unsalted butter, melted

Method:
1. Season the chicken with the garlic powder, onion powder, salt, and pepper.
2. Take Ninja Foodi multi-cooker, arrange it over a cooking platform, and open the top lid.
3. In the pot, add the water. Arrange reversible rack and place the Crisping Basket over the rack. Add the chicken in the basket. Seal the multi-cooker by locking it with the pressure lid; ensure to keep the pressure release valve locked/sealed.
4. Select "PRESSURE" mode and select the "HI" pressure level. Then, set timer to 25 minutes and press "STOP/START"; it will start the cooking process by building up inside pressure.
5. When the timer goes off, naturally release inside pressure for about 8-10 minutes. Then, quick-release pressure by adjusting the pressure valve to the VENT.
6. Brush the chicken with the butter. Season lightly with more salt and pepper. Seal the multi-cooker by locking it with the crisping lid; ensure to keep the pressure release valve locked/sealed.
7. Select the "AIR CRISP" mode and adjust the 400°F temperature level. Then, set timer to 15 minutes and press "STOP/START"; it will start the cooking process by building up inside pressure.
8. When the timer goes off, quick release pressure by adjusting the pressure valve to the VENT. After pressure gets released, open the pressure lid. Slice the chicken and serve warm.

Nutritional Values (Per Serving):
Calories: 439 Fat: 28.5g Saturated Fat: 2.5g Trans Fat: 0g Carbohydrates: 3g Fiber: 0.5g Sodium: 657mg Protein: 40g

Cream Tomato Chicken

Prep Time: 5-10 min.
Cooking Time: 17 min.
Number of Servings: 6

Ingredients:
- 1 garlic clove, grated
- 2 tablespoons garam masala
- 1 tablespoon unsalted butter
- 1 onion, chopped
- ¼ cup tomato paste
- ½ teaspoon cayenne pepper or paprika
- Black pepper (ground) and salt to taste
- 1 pound chicken breast, cut into cubes
- 1 cup heavy (whipping) cream
- Fresh cilantro, chopped, for garnish (optional

Method:
1. Take Ninja Foodi multi-cooker, arrange it over a cooking platform, and open the top lid.
2. In the pot, add the butter; Select "SEAR/SAUTÉ" mode and select "MD: HI" pressure level.
3. Press "STOP/START." After about 4-5 minutes, the butter will melt. Add the onions and cook (while stirring) until they become softened and translucent for 3-4 minutes.
4. Add the garlic, garam masala, more salt, pepper to taste, cayenne pepper, and tomato paste — Stir Cook for 2-3 minutes.
5. Add the heavy cream and combine. Add the chicken and season with salt and pepper.
6. Seal the multi-cooker by locking it with the pressure lid; ensure to keep the pressure release valve locked/sealed.
7. Select "PRESSURE" mode and select the "HI" pressure level. Then, set timer to 10 minutes and press "STOP/START"; it will start the cooking process by building up inside pressure.
8. When the timer goes off, quick release pressure by adjusting the pressure valve to the VENT. After pressure gets released, open the pressure lid. Serve warm and enjoy!

Nutritional Values (Per Serving):
Calories: 283 Fat: 21g Saturated Fat: 4g Trans Fat: 0g Carbohydrates: 5g Fiber: 1g Sodium: 544mg Protein: 18g

Cauliflower Chicken Meal

Prep Time: 5-10 min.
Cooking Time: 10 min.
Number of Servings: 4

Ingredients:
- 1 teaspoon Creole seasoning
- 2 green bell peppers, deseeded and sliced
- 2 tablespoons olive oil
- 4 chicken breasts, thinly sliced
- Salt to taste
- 1 lemon, zested and juiced
- 1 cup cauliflower florets
- 1 cup chicken broth
- 2 green onions, chopped
- 2 tablespoons chopped parsley

Method:
1. Season, the chicken with Creole seasoning.
2. Take Ninja Foodi multi-cooker, arrange it over a cooking platform, and open the top lid.
3. In the pot, add the oil; Select "SEAR/SAUTÉ" mode and select "MD: HI" pressure level.
4. Press "STOP/START." After about 4-5 minutes, the oil will start simmering.
5. Add the meat, bell peppers, and stir-cook for about 5 minutes to brown evenly. Add the cauliflower, chicken broth, and salt. Combine well.
6. Seal the multi-cooker by locking it with the pressure lid; ensure to keep the pressure release valve locked/sealed.
7. Select "PRESSURE" mode and select the "HI" pressure level. Then, set timer to 4 minutes and press "STOP/START"; it will start the cooking process by building up inside pressure.
8. When the timer goes off, quick release pressure by adjusting the pressure valve to the VENT. After pressure gets released, open the pressure lid. Mix the lemon zest, lemon juice, green onions, and parsley. Serve warm and enjoy!

Nutritional Values (Per Serving):
Calories: 546 Fat: 31.5g Saturated Fat: 4.5g Trans Fat: 0g Carbohydrates: 7g Fiber: 2g Sodium: 854mg Protein: 49g

Garlic And Lemon Chicken

Prep Time: 10 minutes
Cooking Time: 30 minutes
Number of Servings: 4

Ingredients:
- 1-2 pounds chicken breast
- 1 teaspoon salt
- 1 onion, diced
- 1 tablespoon ghee
- 5 garlic cloves, minced
- ½ cup organic chicken broth
- 1 teaspoon dried parsley
- 1 large lemon juice
- 3-4 teaspoon arrowroot flour

Method:
1. Set your Ninja Foodi to Saute mode
2. Add diced up the onion and cooking fat
3. Allow the onions to cook for 5 -10 minutes
4. Add the rest of the ingredients except arrowroot flour
5. Lock up the lid and set the pot to poultry mode
6. Cook until the timer runs out
7. Allow the pressure to release naturally
8. Once done, remove ¼ cup of the sauce from the pot and add arrowroot to make a slurry
9. Add the slurry to the pot to make the gravy thick
10. Keep stirring well
11. Serve!

Nutritional Values (Per Serving)
Calories: 462 Fat: 60g Saturated Fat: 12 g Carbohydrates: 5 g Fiber: 2 g Sodium: 382 mg Protein: 51 g

Hassle Chicken

Prep Time: 5 minutes
Cooking Time: 1 hour
Number of Servings: 4

Ingredients:
- 8 large chicken breasts
- 4 large Roma tomatoes, thinly sliced
- 2 cups fresh mozzarella cheese, thinly sliced
- 4 tablespoons butter
- Salt and pepper to taste

Method:
1. Make a few deep slits in your chicken breast
2. Season with salt and pepper
3. Stuff mozzarella cheese slices and tomatoes in chicken slits
4. Grease Ninja Foodi pot with butter
5. Arrange stuffed chicken breasts
6. Lock lid and BAKE/ROAST for 1 hour at 365 degrees F
7. Serve and enjoy!

Nutritional Values (Per Serving)
Calories: 278g Fat: 15g Saturated Fat: 3 g Carbohydrates: 3.9g Fiber: 1 g Sodium: 409 mg Protein: 15g

Chapter 4: Fish And Seafood Recipes

Cool Sweet Fish

Prep Time: 10 minutes
Cooking Time: 6 minutes
Number of Servings: 4

Ingredients:
- 1 pound fish chunks
- 1 tablespoon vinegar
- 2 drops liquid stevia
- ¼ cup butter
- Salt and pepper to taste

Method:
1. Set your Ninja Foodi to Saute mode
2. Add butter and melt it
3. Add fish chunks, saute for 3 minutes
4. Add stevia, salt, pepper, stir it
5. Close the crisping lid
6. Cook on "Air Crisp" mode for 3 minutes to 360 degrees F
7. Serve and enjoy!

Nutritional Values (Per Serving)
Calories: 274g Fat: 15g Saturated Fat: 4 g Carbohydrates: 2g Fiber: 0 g Sodium: 896 mg Protein: 33g

Shrimp Zoodles

Prep Time: 10 minutes
Cooking Time: 3 minutes
Number of Servings: 4

Ingredients:
- 4 cups zoodles
- 1 tablespoon basil, chopped
- 2 tablespoons Ghee
- 1 cup vegetable stock
- 2 garlic cloves, minced
- 2 tablespoons olive oil
- ½ lemon
- ½ teaspoon paprika

Method:
1. Set your Ninja Foodi to Saute mode and add ghee, let it heat up
2. Add olive oil as well
3. Add garlic and cook for 1 minute
4. Add lemon juice, shrimp and cook for 1 minute
5. Stir in rest of the ingredients and lock lid, cook on LOW pressure for 5 minutes
6. Quick-release pressure and serve
7. Enjoy!

Nutritional Values (Per Serving)
Calories: 277 Fat: 6g Saturated Fat: 2 g Carbohydrates: 5 g Fiber: 1 g Sodium: 980 mg Protein: 27 g

Easy Fish Stew

Prep Time: 5 minutes
Cooking Time: 20 minutes
Number of Servings: 4

Ingredients:
- 1 pound white fish fillets, chopped
- 1 cup broccoli, chopped
- 3 cups fish stock
- 1 onion, diced
- 2 cups celery stalks, chopped
- 1 cup heavy cream
- 1 bay leaf
-
- 1 and ½ cups cauliflower, diced
- 1 carrot, sliced
- 2 tablespoons butter
- ¼ teaspoon garlic powder
- ½ teaspoon salt
- ¼ teaspoon pepper

Method:
1. Set your Ninja Foodi to Saute mode
2. Add butter, and let it melt
3. Add onion and carrots, cook for 3 minutes
4. Stir in remaning ingredients
5. Close the lid
6. Cook for 4 monutes on High
7. Release the pressure naturally over 10 minutes
8. Remove the bay leave once cooked
9. Serve and enjoy!

Nutritional Values (Per Serving)
Calories: 298g Fat: 18g Saturated Fat: 3 g Carbohydrates: 6g Fiber: 2 g Sodium: 846 mg Protein: 24g

Buttery Scallops

Prep Time: 10 minutes
Cooking Time: 5 minutes
Number of Servings: 4

Ingredients:
- 2 pounds sea scallops
- 12 cup butter
- 4 garlic cloves, minced
- 4 tablespoons rosemary, chopped
- Salt and pepper to taste

Method:
1. Set your Ninja Foodi to saute mode
2. Add rosemary, garlic and butter, saute for 1 minute
3. Add scallops, salt and pepper, saute for 2 minutes
4. Close the crisping lid
5. Cook for 3 minutes to 350 degree F
6. Serve and enjoy!

Nutritional Values (Per Serving)
Calories: 278g Fat: 15g Saturated Fat: 4 g Carbohydrates: 5g Fiber: 2 g Sodium: 502 mg Protein: 25g

Lovely Air Fried Scallops

Prep Time: 5 minutes
Cooking Time: 5 minutes
Number of Servings: 4

Ingredients:

- 12 scallops
- 3 tablespoons olive oil
- Salt and pepper, to taste

Method:

1. Rub the scallops with salt, pepper and olive oil
2. Transfer it to Ninja foodi
3. Place the insert in your Ninja foodi
4. Close the air crisping lid
5. Cook for 4 minutes to 390 degree F
6. Flip them after 2 minutes
7. Serve and enjoy!

Nutritional Values (Per Serving)

Calories: 372g Fat: 11g Saturated Fat: 3 g Carbohydrates: 0.9g Fiber: 0 g Sodium: 750 mg Protein: 63g

Sweet And Sour Fish

Prep Time: 10 minutes
Cooking Time: 6 minutes
Number of Servings: 4

Ingredients:
- 1 pound fish chunks
- 1 tablespoon vinegar
- 2 drops liquid stevia
- ¼ cup butter
- Salt and pepper to taste

Method:
1. Set your Ninja Foodi to Saute mode
2. Add butter and melt it
3. Add fish chunks, saute for 3 minutes
4. Add stevia, salt, pepper, stir it
5. Close the crisping lid
6. Cook on "Air Crisp" mode for 3 minutes to 360 degree F
7. Serve and enjoy!

Nutritional Values (Per Serving)
Calories: 274g Fat: 15g Saturated Fat: 4 g Carbohydrates: 2g Fiber: 0 g Sodium: 896 mg Protein: 33g

Panko Cod Delight

Prep Time: 10 minutes
Cooking Time: 15 minutes
Number of Servings: 4

Ingredients:
- 2 uncooked cod fillets, 6 ounces each
- 3 teaspoons kosher salt
- ¾ cup panko bread crumbs
- 2 tablespoons butter, melted
- ¼ cup fresh parsley, minced
- 1 lemon. Zested and juiced

Method:
1. Pre-heat your Ninja Foodi at 390 degrees F and place Air Crisper basket inside
2. Season cod and salt
3. Take a bowl and add bread crumbs, parsley, lemon juice, zest, butter, and mix well
4. Coat fillets with the bread crumbs mixture and place fillets in your Air Crisping basket
5. Lock Air Crisping lid and cook on Air Crisp mode for 15 minutes at 360 degrees F
6. Serve and enjoy!

Nutritional Values (Per Serving)
Calories: 554 Fat: 24g Saturated Fat: 12 g Carbohydrates: 5 g Fiber: 2 g Sodium: 532 mg Protein: 37 g

Salmon And Kale Meal

Prep Time: 10 minutes
Cooking Time: 5 minutes
Number of Servings: 4

Ingredients:

- 1 lemon, juiced
- 2 salmon fillets
- ¼ cup extra virgin olive oil
- 1 teaspoon Dijon mustard
- 4 cups kale, thinly sliced, ribs removed
- 1 teaspoon salt
- 1 avocado, diced
- 1 cup pomegranate seeds
- 1 cup walnuts, toasted
- 1 cup goat parmesan cheese, shredded

Method:

1. Season salmon with salt and keep it on the side
2. Place a trivet in your Ninja Foodi
3. Place salmon over the trivet
4. Lock lid and cook on HIGH pressure for 15 minutes
5. Release pressure naturally over 10 minutes
6. Transfer salmon to a serving platter
7. Take a bowl and add kale, season with salt
8. Take another bowl and make the dressing by adding lemon juice, Dijon mustard, olive oil, and red wine vinegar
9. Season kale with dressing and add diced avocado, pomegranate seeds, walnuts and cheese
10. Toss and serve with the fish
11. Enjoy!

Nutritional Values (Per Serving)

Calories: 234 Fat: 14g Saturated Fat: 6 g Carbohydrates: 12 g Fiber: 2 g Sodium: 118 mg Protein: 16 g

Lemon And Garlic Flavored Prawn Dish

Prep Time: 5 minutes
Cooking Time: 5 minutes
Number of Servings: 4

Ingredients:
- 1 pound prawns
- 2/3 cup fish stock
- 1 tablespoon butter
- 2 tablespoons olive oil
- 2 tablespoons garlic, minced
- 2 tablespoons lemon juice
- 1 tablespoon lemon zest
- Salt and pepper to taste

Method:
1. Set your Ninja Foodi to Saute mode
2. Add oil and butter, let it heat up
3. Stir in remaining ingredients
4. Close the lid
5. Cook for 5 minutes on LOW
6. Quick-release the pressure
7. Serve and enjoy!

Nutritional Values (Per Serving)
Calories: 236g Fat: 12g Saturated Fat: 3 g Carbohydrates: 2g Fiber: 1 g Sodium: 964 mg Protein: 27g

Chapter 5: Beef And Lamb Recipes

Mustard Dreged Pork

Prep Time: 10 minutes
Cooking Time: 30 minutes
Number of Servings: 4

Ingredients:
- 2 tablespoons ghee
- 2 tablespoons Dijon mustard
- 4 pork chops
- Salt and pepper to taste
- 1 tablespoon fresh rosemary, coarsely chopped

Method:
1. Take a bowl and add pork chops, cover with Dijon mustard and carefully sprinkle rosemary, salt, and pepper
2. Let it marinate for 2 hours
3. Add ghee and marinated pork chops to your Ninja Foodi pot
4. Lock lid and cook on Low-Medium Pressure for 30 minutes
5. Release pressure naturally over 10 minutes
6. Take the dish out, serve, and enjoy!

Nutritional Values (Per Serving)
Calories: 315 Fat: 26g Saturated Fat: 8 g Carbohydrates: 1g Fiber: 0 g Sodium: 199 mg Protein: 18g

Jamaican Pork Dish

Prep Time: 10 minutes
Cooking Time: 45 minutes
Number of Servings: 4

Ingredients:
- ½ cup beef stock
- 1 tablespoon olive oil
- ¼ cup Jamaican jerk spice blend
- 4 ounces of pork shoulder

Method:
1. Rub roast with olive oil and spice blend
2. Set your Ninja Foodi to Saute mode and add meat, brown all sides
3. Pour beef broth
4. Lock lid and cook on HIGH pressure for 45 minutes
5. Quick-release pressure
6. Shred pork and serve!

Nutritional Values (Per Serving)
Calories: 308 Fat: 18g Saturated Fat: 6 g Carbohydrates: 5 g Fiber: 3 g Sodium: 210 mg Protein: 31 g

Tantalizing Beef Jerky

Prep Time: 10 minutes
Cooking Time: 20 minutes
Number of Servings: 4

Ingredients:
- ½ pound beef, sliced into 1/8 inch thick strips
- 2 tablespoons Worcestershire sauce
- 1 teaspoon onion powder
- ½ cup of soy sauce
- ½ teaspoon garlic powder
- 1 teaspoon salt
- 2 teaspoons ground black pepper

Method:
1. Take a large-sized ziplock bag and add all the ingredients
2. Seal it shut
3. Shake well and leave it in the fridge overnight
4. Lay strips on dehydrator trays, let not overlap them
5. Close the air crisping lid
6. Cook for 20 minutes to 135 degree F
7. Serve and enjoy!

Nutritional Values (Per Serving)
Calories: 62 Fat: 7g Saturated Fat: 2 g Carbohydrates: 2g Fiber: 0 g Sodium: 447 mg Protein: 9g

Spicy Adobo Steak

Prep Time: 5 minutes
Cooking Time: 25 minutes
Number of Servings: 4

Ingredients:

- 2 cups of water
- 8 steaks, cubed, 28 ounces pack
- Pepper to taste
- 1 and ¾ teaspoons adobo seasoning
- 1 can (8 ounces) tomato sauce
- 1/3 cup green pitted olives
- 2 tablespoons brine
- 1 small red pepper
- ½ a medium onion, sliced

Method:

1. Chop onions and peppers into ¼ inch strips
2. Season the beef with pepper and adobo
3. Add into Ninja Foodi
4. Add remaining ingredients and close the lid
5. Cook for 25 minutes on HIGH
6. Release pressure naturally
7. Serve and enjoy!

Nutritional Values (Per Serving)

Calories: 154 Fat: 5g Saturated Fat: 1 g Carbohydrates: 3g Fiber: 1 g Sodium: 700 mg Protein: 23g

Beef Stew

Prep Time: 10 minutes
Cooking Time: 10 minutes
Number of Servings: 4

Ingredients:
- 1 pound beef roast
- 4 cups beef broth
- 2 tomatoes, chopped
- ½ white onion, chopped
- 3 garlic cloves, chopped
- 1 carrot, chopped
- 2 celery stalks, chopped
- ¼ teaspoon salt
- 1/8 teaspoon ground black pepper

Method:
1. Add all ingredients to your Ninja Foodi
2. Close the lid
3. Cook for 10 minutes on HIGH
4. Quick release pressure
5. Once cooked open the lid and shred the beef using forks
6. Serve and enjoy!

Nutritional Values (Per Serving)
Calories: 211 Fat: 7g Saturated Fat: 2 g Carbohydrates: 2g Fiber: 0 g Sodium: 546 mg Protein: 10g

Lamb Roast

Prep Time: 10 minutes
Cooking Time: 60 minutes
Number of Servings: 4

Ingredients:
- 2 pounds lamb roasted Wegmans
- 1 cup beef broth
- 1 cup onion soup
- Salt and pepper to taste

Method:
1. Place your lamb roast to your Ninja Foodi pot
2. Add beef broth, onion soup, salt and pepper
3. Close the lid
4. Cook for 55 minutes on Medium-HIGH
5. Release pressure naturally over 10 minutes
6. Serve and enjoy!

Nutritional Values (Per Serving)

Calories: 211 Fat: 7g Saturated Fat: 2 g Carbohydrates: 2g Fiber: 1 g Sodium: 325 mg Protein: 10g

Mustard Pork

Prep Time: 10 minutes
Cooking Time: 30 minutes
Number of Servings: 4

Ingredients:
- 2 tablespoons ghee
- 2 tablespoons Dijon mustard
- 4 pork chops
- Salt and pepper to taste
- 1 tablespoon fresh rosemary, coarsely chopped

Method:
1. Take a bowl and add pork chops, cover with Dijon mustard and carefully sprinkle rosemary, salt, and pepper
2. Let it marinate for 2 hours
3. Add ghee and marinated pork chops to your Ninja Foodi pot
4. Lock lid and cook on Low-Medium Pressure for 30 minutes
5. Release pressure naturally over 10 minutes
6. Take the dish out, serve and enjoy!

Nutritional Values (Per Serving)
Calories: 315 Fat: 26g Saturated Fat: 8 g Carbohydrates: 1g Fiber: 0 g Sodium: 199 mg Protein: 18g

Deliciously Smothered Pork Chops

Prep Time: 10 minutes
Cooking Time: 28 minutes
Number of Servings: 4

Ingredients:
- 6 ounce of boneless pork loin chops
- 1 tablespoon of paprika
- 1 teaspoon of garlic powder
- 1 teaspoon of onion powder
- 1 teaspoon of black pepper
- 1 teaspoon of salt
- ¼ teaspoon of cayenne pepper
- 2 tablespoon of coconut oil
- ½ of a sliced medium onion
- 6-ounce baby Bella mushrooms, sliced
- 1 tablespoon of butter
- ½ a cup of whip cream
- ¼ teaspoon of xanthan gum
- 1 tablespoon parsley, chopped

Method:
1. Take a small bowl and add garlic powder, paprika, onion powder, black pepper, salt, and cayenne pepper
2. Rinse the pork chops and pat them dry
3. Sprinkle both sides with 1 teaspoon of the mixture making sure to rub the seasoning all over the meat
4. Reserve the remaining spice
5. Set your Ninja Foodi to Saute mode and add coconut oil, allow the oil to heat up
6. Brown the chops 3 minutes per sides
7. Remove and cancel the Saute mode
8. Add sliced onion to the base of your pot alongside mushrooms
9. Top with the browned pork chops
10. Lock up the lid and cook on HIGH pressure for 25 minutes
11. Release the pressure naturally over 10 minutes, remove the pork chops and keep them on a plate
12. Set your pot to Saute mode and whisk in remaining spices mix, heavy cream, and butter
13. Sprinkle ¼ teaspoon of xanthan gum and stir
14. Simmer for 3-5 minutes and remove the heat
15. Add a bit more xanthan gum if you require a heavier gravy
16. Top the pork chops with the gravy and sprinkle parsley
17. Serve!

Nutritional Values (Per Serving)
Calories: 481 Fat: 32g Saturated Fat: 15 g Carbohydrates: 6 g Fiber: 2 g Sodium: 210 mg Protein: 39 g

Beef And Broccoli Meal

Prep Time: 10 minutes
Cooking Time: 15 minutes
Number of Servings: 4

Ingredients:

- 1 and ½ pounds beef round steak, cut into 2 inches by 1/8 inch strips
- 1 cup broccoli, diced
- ½ teaspoon red pepper flakes
- 2 teaspoon garlic, minced
- 2 teaspoons olive oil
- 2 tablespoons apple cider vinegar
- 2 tablespoons coconut aminos
- 2 tablespoons white wine vinegar
- 1 tablespoons arrowroot
- ¼ cup beef broth

Method:

1. Take a large-sized bowl and make the sauce by mixing in red pepper flakes, olive oil, coconut aminos, garlic, white wine vinegar, apple cider vinegar, broth and arrowroot
2. Mix well
3. Add the mix to your Ninja Foodi
4. Add beef and place a lid
5. Cook on SLOW COOK MODE (LOW) for 6-8 hours
6. Uncover just 30 minutes before end time and add broccoli, lock lid again and let it finish
7. Serve and enjoy!

Nutritional Values (Per Serving)

Calories: 208 Fat: 12g Saturated Fat: 14 g Carbohydrates: 11 g Fiber: 3 g Sodium: 545 mg Protein: 15 g

Hearty New York Strip

Prep Time: 10 minutes
Cooking Time: 9 minutes
Number of Servings: 4

Ingredients:
- 24 ounces NY strip steak
- ½ teaspoon ground black pepper
- 1 teaspoon salt

Method:
1. Add steaks on a metal trivet, place it on your Ninja Foodi
2. Season with salt and pepper
3. Add 1 cup water to the pot
4. Close the lid
5. Cook for 1 minute on HIGH
6. Quick-release pressure
7. Place Air-crisp lid and Air Crisp for 8 minutes for a medium-steak
8. Serve and enjoy!

Nutritional Values (Per Serving)
Calories: 503 Fat: 46g Saturated Fat: 12 g Carbohydrates: 1g Fiber: 0 g Sodium: 715 mg Protein: 46g

Chapter 6: Dessert

Simple Poached Pears

Prep Time: 5 minutes
Cooking Time: 10 minutes
Number of Servings: 6

Ingredients:

- 6 firm pears, peeled
- 4 garlic cloves, minced
- 1 stick cinnamon
- 1 fresh ginger, minced
- 1 bottle of dry red wine
- 1 bay leaf
- Mixed Italian herbs as needed
- 1 and 1/3 cups stevia

Method:

1. Peel the pears leaving the stems attached
2. Pour wine into your Ninja Foodi
3. Add cinnamon, cloves, ginger, bay leaf, and stevia, stir gently
4. Add pears to the pot
5. Close the lid
6. Cook for 9 minutes on HIGH
7. Quick-release the pressure
8. Take the pears out using a tong, keep them on the side
9. Set Saute mode, make the mixture into half
10. Drizzle the mixture with pears
11. Serve and enjoy!

Nutritional Values (Per Serving)

Calories: 150 Fat: 16g Saturated Fat: 4 g Carbohydrates: 2g Fiber: 0 g Sodium: 13 mg Protein: 0.5g

Buttery Fennel And Garlic

Prep Time: 10 minutes
Cooking Time: 5 minutes
Number of Servings: 4

Ingredients:
- ½ stick butter
- 2 garlic cloves, sliced
- ½ teaspoon salt
- 1 and ½ pounds fennel bulbs, cut into wedges
- ¼ teaspoon ground black pepper
- ½ teaspoon cayenne
- ¼ teaspoon dried dill weed
- 1/3 cup dry white wine
- 2/3 cup stock

Method:
1. Set your Ninja Foodi to Saute mode and add butter, let it heat up
2. Add garlic and cook for 30 seconds
3. Add rest of the ingredients
4. Lock lid and cook on LOW pressure for 3 minutes
5. Remove lid and serve
6. Enjoy!

Nutritional Values (Per Serving)
Calories: 111 Fat: 6g Saturated Fat: 2 g Carbohydrates: 2 g Fiber: 2 g Sodium: 317 mg Protein: 2 g

Cheesy Cauliflower Steak

Prep Time: 10 minutes
Cooking Time: 30 minutes
Number of Servings: 4

Ingredients:
- 1 tablespoon mustard
- 1 head cauliflower
- 1 teaspoon avocado mayonnaise
- ½ cup parmesan cheese, grated
- ¼ cup butter, cut into small pieces

Method:
1. Set your Ninja Foodi to Saute mode and add butter and cauliflower
2. Saute for 3 minutes
3. Add remaining ingredients and stir
4. Lock lid and cook on HIGH pressure for 30 minutes
5. Release pressure naturally over 10 minutes
6. Serve and enjoy!

Nutritional Values (Per Serving)
Calories: 155 Fat: 13g Saturated Fat: 2 g Carbohydrates: 4 g Fiber: 2 g Sodium: 162 mg Protein: 6 g

Garlic And Mushroom Munchies

Prep Time: 10 minutes
Cooking Time: 8 hours
Number of Servings: 4

Ingredients:
- ¼ cup vegetable stock
- 2 tablespoons extra virgin olive oil
- 1 tablespoon Dijon mustard
- 1 teaspoon dried thyme
- 1 teaspoon of sea salt
- ½ teaspoon dried rosemary
- ¼ teaspoon fresh ground black pepper
- 2 pounds cremini mushrooms, cleaned
- 6 garlic cloves, minced
- ¼ cup fresh parsley, chopped

Method:
1. Take a small bowl and whisk in vegetable stock, mustard, olive oil, salt, thyme, pepper and rosemary
2. Add mushrooms, garlic and stock mix to your Ninja Foodi
3. Close lid and cook on SLOW COOK Mode (LOW) for 8 hours
4. Open the lid and stir in parsley
5. Serve and enjoy!

Nutritional Values (Per Serving)
Calories: 92 Fat: 5g Saturated Fat: 2 g Carbohydrates: 8 g Fiber: 2 g Sodium: 550 mg Protein: 4 g

Warm Glazed Up Carrots

Prep Time: 5 minutes
Cooking Time: 5 minutes
Number of Servings: 4

Ingredients:
- 2 pounds carrots
- Pepper as needed
- 1 cup of water
- 1 tablespoon coconut butter

Method:
1. Wash carrots thoroughly and peel then, slice the carrots
2. Add carrots, water to the Ninja Foodi
3. Lock pressure lid and cook for 4 minutes on HIGH pressure
4. Release pressure naturally
5. Strain carrots and strain carrots
6. Mix with coconut butter, enjoy with a bit of pepper

Nutritional Values (Per Serving)
Calories: 228 Fat: 8g Saturated Fat: 2 g Carbohydrates: 36g Fiber: 2 g Sodium: 123 mg Protein: 4g

Chapter 7: Appetizers & Sides

Cauliflower Cheddar

Prep Time: 5-10 min.   **Cooking Time: 6 min.**   **Number of Servings: 4**

Ingredients:
- ½ cup chicken broth
- Black pepper (ground) and salt to taste
- ½ cup heavy cream
- 2 medium cauliflower, cut into small florets
- ½ teaspoon garlic powder
- ½ teaspoon onion powder
- 1 cup grated cheddar cheese
- ¼ cup grated Gruyere cheese
- 1 tablespoon chopped parsley

Method:
1. Take Ninja Foodi multi-cooker, arrange it over a cooking platform, and open the top lid.
2. In the pot, add the cauliflower, garlic powder, onion powder, chicken broth, salt, and black pepper. Stir well.
3. Seal the multi-cooker by locking it with the pressure lid; ensure to keep the pressure release valve locked/sealed.
4. Select "PRESSURE" mode and select the "HI" pressure level. Then, set timer to 3 minutes and press "STOP/START"; it will start the cooking process by building up inside pressure.
5. When the timer goes off, quick release pressure by adjusting the pressure valve to the VENT. After pressure gets released, open the pressure lid.
6. Select "SEAR/SAUTÉ" mode and select the "MD" pressure level; add the cream and cheese and combine. Stir-cook for 3-4 minutes.
7. Serve warm with the parsley on top and enjoy!

Nutritional Values (Per Serving):
Calories: 339   Fat: 31.5g   Saturated Fat: 8g   Trans Fat: 0g   Carbohydrates: 6g   Fiber: 2g   Sodium: 223mg   Protein: 6g

Bacon Green Beans

Prep Time: 5-10 min.
Cooking Time: 9 min.
Number of Servings: 4

Ingredients:

- 1 ½ cups green beans
- 6 tablespoons vegetable broth
- Black pepper (ground) and salt to taste
- 1/4 teaspoon red chili flakes
- 3 bacon slices, chopped
- 2 garlic cloves, minced
- 2 teaspoons lemon juice

Method:

1. Take Ninja Foodi multi-cooker, arrange it over a cooking platform, and open the top lid. Select "SEAR/SAUTÉ" mode and select "MD: HI" pressure level.
2. Press "STOP/START." After about 4-5 minutes, the unit will be heated up.
3. Add the bacon in the pot and stir-cook until turn evenly crispy for 4-5 minutes. Drain over a paper towel and set aside.
4. Add the garlic in the pot and cook (while stirring) until it becomes fragrant and translucent. Add the green beans, vegetable broth, salt, black pepper, and red chili flakes; stir the mixture.
5. Seal the multi-cooker by locking it with the pressure lid; ensure to keep the pressure release valve locked/sealed.
6. Select "PRESSURE" mode and select the "HI" pressure level. Then, set timer to 4 minutes and press "STOP/START"; it will start the cooking process by building up inside pressure.
7. When the timer goes off, quick release pressure by adjusting the pressure valve to the VENT. After pressure gets released, open the pressure lid. Serve warm with the lemon juice and bacon on top.

Nutritional Values (Per Serving):

Calories: 163 Fat: 11.5g Saturated Fat: 4g Trans Fat: 0g Carbohydrates: 5g Fiber: 0.5g Sodium: 257mg Protein: 4g

Zucchini Crisp

Prep Time: 5-10 min.
Cooking Time: 20 min.
Number of Servings: 4

Ingredients:
- 1 tablespoon garlic powder
- ¼ teaspoon red pepper flakes
- 1 teaspoon dried oregano
- 1 cup almond flour
- ¼ cup grated Parmesan cheese
- Freshly ground black pepper and salt to taste
- 2 eggs, beaten
- 3 large zucchini, cut into sticks

Method:
1. In a mixing bowl, add the almond flour, Parmesan cheese, garlic powder, red pepper flakes, oregano, salt, and pepper. Combine the ingredients to mix well with each other.
2. In a mixing bowl, beat the eggs. Coat the zucchini sticks with the egg mixture and then coat with the flour mixture.
3. Take Ninja Foodi multi-cooker, arrange it over a cooking platform, and open the top lid.
4. In the pot, arrange a reversible rack and place the Crisping Basket over the rack.
5. In the basket, add the zucchini sticks.
6. Seal the multi-cooker by locking it with the crisping lid; ensure to keep the pressure release valve locked/sealed.
7. Select the "AIR CRISP" mode and adjust the 375°F temperature level. Then, set timer to 20 minutes and press "STOP/START"; it will start the cooking process by building up inside pressure. Shake the basket after 10 minutes.
8. When the timer goes off, quick release pressure by adjusting the pressure valve to the VENT.
9. After pressure gets released, open the pressure lid. Serve warm and enjoy!

Nutritional Values (Per Serving):
Calories: 223   Fat: 13.5g   Saturated Fat: 2g   Trans Fat: 0g   Carbohydrates: 10g   Fiber: 34g   Sodium: 527mg   Protein: 12.5g

Butter Brussels Sprouts

Prep Time: 5-10 min.
Cooking Time: 3 min.
Number of Servings: 4

Ingredients:
- 2 tablespoon. melted butter
- Salt to taste
- 2 cups Brussels sprouts
- 1 lemon, juiced

Method:
1. Take Ninja Foodi multi-cooker, arrange it over a cooking platform, and open the top lid.
2. In the pot, add the 1 cup water. Take Crisping Basket and add the broccoli. Place the basket in the pot.
3. Seal the multi-cooker by locking it with the pressure lid; ensure to keep the pressure release valve locked/sealed.
4. Select "PRESSURE" mode and select the "HI" pressure level. Then, set timer to 3 minutes and press "STOP/START"; it will start the cooking process by building up inside pressure.
5. When the timer goes off, quick release pressure by adjusting the pressure valve to the VENT. After pressure gets released, open the pressure lid.
6. Add the broccoli into a mixing bowl; add the lemon juice, butter, and salt. Combine and serve warm.

Nutritional Values (Per Serving):
Calories: 394 Fat: 15.5g Saturated Fat: 1.5g Trans Fat: 0g Carbohydrates: 5g Fiber: 1.5g Sodium: 246mg Protein: 23g

Parmesan Squash

Prep Time: 5-10 min.
Cooking Time: 8 min.
Number of Servings: 4

Ingredients:

- ½ tablespoon garlic powder
- ¼ teaspoon red pepper flakes (optional)
- 2 tablespoons extra-virgin olive oil
- 2 tablespoons grated Parmesan cheese
- 4 summer squash, trimmed and sliced
- Black pepper (ground) and salt to taste
- 3 tablespoons chopped fresh basil or parsley, for garnish

Method:

1. Season the squash with the garlic powder, red pepper flakes, salt, and black pepper.
2. Take Ninja Foodi multi-cooker, arrange it over a cooking platform, and open the top lid.
3. In the pot, add the oil; Select "SEAR/SAUTÉ" mode and select "MD: HI" pressure level. Press "STOP/START." After about 4-5 minutes, the oil will start simmering.
4. Add the onions and cook (while stirring) until they become softened and translucent.
5. Add the squash and stir-cook until turn tender for 4-5 minutes. Sprinkle with the Parmesan cheese.
6. Seal the multi-cooker by locking it with the crisping lid; ensure to keep the pressure release valve locked/sealed.
7. Select "BROIL" mode and select the "HI" pressure level. Then, set timer to 4 minutes and press "STOP/START"; it will start the cooking process by building up inside pressure.
8. When the timer goes off, quick release pressure by adjusting the pressure valve to the VENT.
9. After pressure gets released, open the pressure lid. Serve warm with the basil on top and enjoy!

Nutritional Values (Per Serving):

Calories: 134 Fat: 9.5g Saturated Fat: 1g Trans Fat: 0g Carbohydrates: 7g Fiber: 2g Sodium: 423mg Protein: 4g

Chapter 8: Dessert

Decadent Lemon Mousse

Prep Time: 10 minutes
Cooking Time: 12 minutes
Number of Servings: 2

Ingredients:
- 1-2 ounces cream cheese, soft
- ½ teaspoon lemon liquid stevia
- ½ cup heavy cream
- 1/8 cup fresh lemon juice
- 2 pinch salt

Method:
1. In a bowl add heavy cream, cream cheese, stevia, lemon juice and salt
2. Pour the mixture into a ramekin and transfer to Ninja foodi
3. Close the lid
4. Set Bake/Roast mode
5. Bake for 12 minutes to 350 degree F
6. Check the doneness it before remove from the Ninja Foodi
7. Serve and enjoy!

Nutritional Values (Per Serving)
Calories: 292 Fat: 26g Saturated Fat: 8 g Carbohydrates: 8g Fiber: 1 g Sodium: 30 mg Protein: 5g

Pumpkin Carrot Pudding

Prep Time: 10 minutes
Cooking Time: 20 minutes
Number of Servings: 2

Ingredients:

- 2 cups pumpkin, pureed
- 2 cups carrots, shredded
- 2 whole eggs
- 1 tablespoon granulated Erythritol
- 1 teaspoon ground nutmeg
- 1 tablespoon extra-virgin olive oil
- ½ sweet onion, finely chopped
- 1 cup heavy whip cream
- ½ cup cream cheese, soft
- ¼ cup pumpkin seeds, garnish
- ¼ cup water
- ½ teaspoon salt

Method:

1. Add oil to your Ninja Foodi pot and whisk in pumpkin, carrots, heavy cream, cream cheese, eggs, erythritol, onion, nutmeg, water and salt
2. Stir gently and close the lid
3. Cook for 10 minutes on High
4. Release pressure naturally over 10 minutes
5. Top with the pumpkin seeds
6. Serve and enjoy!

Nutritional Values (Per Serving)

Calories: 239 Fat: 19g Saturated Fat: 4 g Carbohydrates: 7g Fiber: 2 g Sodium: 423 mg Protein: 6g

Awesome Poached Pears

Prep Time: 5 minutes
Cooking Time: 10 minutes
Number of Servings: 6

Ingredients:

- 6 firm pears, peeled
- 4 garlic cloves, minced
- 1 stick cinnamon
- 1 fresh ginger, minced
- 1 bottle of dry red wine
- 1 bay leaf
- Mixed Italian herbs as needed
- 1 and 1/3 cups stevia

Method:

1. Peel the pears leaving the stems attached
2. Pour wine into your Ninja Foodi
3. Add cinnamon, cloves, ginger, bay leaf and stevia, stir gently
4. Add pears to the pot
5. Close the lid
6. Cook for 9 minutes on HIGH
7. Quick release the pressure
8. Take the pears out using tong, keep them on the side
9. Set Saute mode, make the mixture into half
10. Drizzle the mixture with pears
11. Serve and enjoy!

Nutritional Values (Per Serving)

Calories: 150 Fat: 16g Saturated Fat: 4 g Carbohydrates: 2g Fiber: 0 g Sodium: 13 mg Protein: 0.5g

www.ingramcontent.com/pod-product-compliance
Lightning Source LLC
Chambersburg PA
CBHW081126080526
44587CB00021B/3762